# COVID: THE WORDY WILDS
# OF A MIND UNDER LOCKDOWN

N. CHAMCHOUN

Covid: The Wordy Wilds of a Mind Under Lockdown
published in the United Kingdom in 2022
by Mica Press

c/o Leslie Bell
47 Belle Vue Road, Wivenhoe, Colchester, Essex CO7 9LD
www.micapress.co.uk | books@micapress.co.uk
www.campanulabooks.uk | info@campanulabooks.uk

ISBN 978-1-869848-31-6

© N. Chamchoun 2022

The right of N. Chamchoun to be identified as the author of this work has been asserted by her in accordance with the Copyright, Designs and Patents Act of 1988.

All rights reserved.

# Contents

pages

| | |
|---|---|
| No Filter | 1 |
| On The Grind | 3 |
| Mama's Welcome | 4 |
| Graduation | 6 |
| Panic! | 7 |
| Breaking! | 8 |
| Ants | 9 |
| A Good Book | 11 |
| Mother and Son | 12 |
| The Imposter | 13 |
| Ode to a Bicycle | 14 |
| Breasts | 15 |
| Lil Big Man | 17 |
| Equilibrium | 18 |
| Grand Union Canal | 19 |
| The Unmoored Moor | 20 |
| Tired | 21 |
| Melancholy | 22 |
| I Have Loved | 23 |
| Father | 24 |
| Sick City | 25 |
| Mapping the Void | 26 |
| The Bat and the Ball | 27 |
| Limbo | 28 |
| The Days | 32 |
| Christmas Present | 33 |
| The Tate | 35 |
| Diluted | 36 |
| When They Were Young | 38 |
| Reconciliation | 40 |
| I Am Not Berber | 42 |
| Where the Birds Don't Fly | 44 |
| Round Trip | 45 |
| Brewing Over a Brew | 47 |
| Resurfacing | 48 |
| Aunty | 49 |
| Garden View | 51 |
| Venus de la Menopausia | 53 |
| Sister | 54 |
| Writing on Reefer | 55 |
| Foodbank | 56 |
| Clocking Out Mum | 58 |

## NO FILTER

This is me; here I sit
growing into my aged jacket
accepting my invisibility.
Rebuking my fragility.

Am I irrelevant?
Wearing my wrinkles as a sackcloth and ashes.
Should I reinvent
myself for the applause
of the social media masses?

Twits twittering on Twitter
showcasing shells on Insta
scrolling and trolling
perfecting personas on FB,
a photoshopping melée.

A veil of airbrushed sadness.
I need more because I am less.
Filtering faces and not words,
subsisting on praises,
captive in "like" cages.

The eyes that don't see me.
The ears that don't hear me.
Should I put on my filter and dance,
to the hollow beat of a digital trance?

A pound of flesh under the knife,
erasing evidence of a lived life.
Fattening up my lips and ass,
a fatted calf, as a stranger
berates me in the looking glass.

Are my eyebrows "on fleek"?
Am I scathingly "savage" enough?
Am I too "woke" or not enough?
I log in and await your critique.

Let's celebrate the cover and not the book.
Post a pic as the panel rates you.
Have an opinion and we hate you,
immersing ourselves in the virtual brook.

I have wandered the London streets
donning my expiry as an invisibility cloak.
As the gaze of the "lit" quickly retreats,
before dissolving into the city's big smoke

I have sat with Eliot as we shared despair.
After shopworn shared niceties.
Over 'tea and cakes and ices'.
Exchanging troughs and peaks as we laughed and cried.
Bitching with Bukowski; waving to Sylvia as we died inside.

Empty voices filling the space with speech
Their flawless faces behind a screen.
Me, out of touch. Them, out of reach.
Where reality and the virtual scheme,
I have haunted the void in-between.

Should I question the truth whilst believing the lie?
The hoards flock to Tik Tok,
Famous for fifteen minutes
to shock, to rock, to mock,
to exhibit without limits.

But I am old and the light in their eyes has died.

## ON THE GRIND

Dressed in threads of adulthood.
Forging the bonds that bind
together in troubled times.
When you can't see past the wood.

Harvesting and investing.
Delayed gratification.
Grafting out of your station.
Consume time without digesting.

Dreams of some day.
Get your foot on the property ladder.
Save on indulgences and work harder.
All work and no play.

Put in the hours to rise.
A promotion or bonus for Jack.
Greasing the cogs to pick up the slack.
Strangled by the tie that ties.

Grind your bones to make his bread.
In a suit suited for ambition.
Silence mental health's attrition.
There is no success for the dead.

Sacrifice for the future.
Feather your pension to cushion the blow.
Retire abroad in a rustic chateau.
Eiderdown for the stupor.

A partner to shoulder the burden.
A mortgage to swallow your labour.
Life's force fuelling the conveyor.
Together, picking out curtains.

## MAMA'S WELCOME

My friend in my home.
Another part of me,
Friends have no secrets.
Billows of ginger and saffron
Embrace our guest at the door.

Mama works in silence in the kitchen.
Even the sound of crockery and cutlery,
Moved by purposeful hands, seems muted.
Conserving the fanfare for the food
Which always sings of Moroccan tradition.

"Where are the knives and forks?"
Quizzes Christine
Glancing around the scene.
"We eat with our hands in one plate."
First horror then a second thought.

A pang of hurt shakes my pride.
Cautiously watching us begin,
Scooping up the food with bread.
She repeats Bismillah and tucks in.
Protruding eyes ecstatically wide.

Hands adapting with ease.
Entranced by flavours unknown.
Hands faster than the throat can swallow.
Remaining, seated; the last to leave.

Mama's smile eclipses her whole face.
Pride radiating, a regal glow.
Mama says, "You're Moroccan now".
Christine's smile welcomes the honour bestowed.
Sharing our respective places
with acceptance and grace.

# GRADUATION

In enforced solitude,
refreshing the interlude.
The river and the ocean
commune at the estuary,
casting down the briny debris
in replenishing motion,
guiding the boat to the quay.

In the eye of memory,
you step, graciously,
into all I knew you to be.
In your black, fur-trimmed, flowing robe.
The mortarboard hat you wore well.
Each warmed chamber swelled,
my eyes, conveying the gratitude owed.

A bud in a concrete estate.
The rocky soil of home.
Determination, honed.
A resolute shine in you.
"You are all you aspire to."
Considering which path to take.

Out of place in the red brick grandeur,
yet adapting with easy charm.
Others drawn to your calm.
I was the teenage mum at the ball.
How far the apple falls.
The patent pride, your presence spurs.

Beaming as you accepted your prize.
Tears of a mother's pride.
The child born to rise.

## PANIC!

Empty shelves.
Our baser selves.
Through the supermarket doors
the peeved, panicked ants pour.

Running the gauntlet
fired up and dauntless,
the grasping, clenching hands.
An eerie exodus of cans.
Entitled and faultless.

The wired scanning eyes
homing in on the prize -
non-perishable goods.
Spillages underfoot.
This little piggy got supplies.

A fragile, anxious stare,
shakily wiping a tear.
Her one day to shop,
in a shop with no stock.
The vulnerable at the rear.
Greed tramples and sneers.

The shelves are pilfered and empty.
One household only allowed entry.
Bulky toilet paper towers
wheeled around as they scour
the pathetic pillaged assembly.
A frothing mob madness.
Checkout beeps of regress.

**BREAKING!**

Channel hopping, disguising the silence outside.
The six o'clock news with expert views.
A floppy-haired harbinger of doom.
A smirking, bungling buffoon.
An assassin's Machiavellian ruse.
Swallowing the bilious contempt inside.

The world's grief oozes in with insidious trepidation.
Salaciously circling the space.
Bringing sadness in its embrace.
Before resting heavily on the heart.

Once, the bereaved brought out their dead.
Today, numbers are broadcast instead.

A car horn breaks the stillness.

Jagged ripples as we break.
Cracking the crippled impotence.
A ghostly, dazed dissonance.
The TV clicks off.
Silence
from the hell that we make.

# ANTS

They're everywhere
they can't be stopped.
Attempts to oust them.
We all complain
recite the same
words as before.

The fixer comes
Laying his traps.
Stop them in their tracks.
"They won't be back."

Then they are gone.
You forget the domination,
the queasy infestation.
A fool's calm.

One day, you notice
the semicolon carcass,
The filar thrashing limbs,
Twitching in the cereal,
rolling in the tea.

You understand
you can't stop them.
They thrive on us.
Hold on to your own.

Sugar, cornflakes
and slice in the fridge.
Give us our daily bread
until the pressure – breaks.

A misery-fuelled rebellion.
The fixer, back to appease.
The illusion of putting out fires.
A placebo for the incursion.

Pull down the wall.
A nest of pestilence
embedded in the structure
built atop human waste.

The rot, tainting us all.

**A GOOD BOOK**

Take flight on the whispered air
of a page gently turned.
Freeing your mind from the here
as reality is adjourned.

The Phileas Fogg of Literature,
cocooned in your ascending balloon.
As reader and writer confer
over the acts of heroes and loons.

Spark up with Dostoyevsky,
with your coffee cups aligned.
revelling in 'the deliciousness
and the bitterness and the addiction'
over the story of time,
a fait accompli.

Ruminating with Rumi
in the mystical Middle East.
Heed the call of Sufis,
Dancing until worries cease.

Stroking the ends as each page turns.
Gobbling the grandeur
as Dante's inferno magnificently burns.
Vibrating as our contentment purrs.

Rolling the projector of the mind.
Plots that entice like a rabbit hole.
A gateway to valour, lost in time.
Predicted futures, full of hyperbole.

A library card passport
to the realms beyond thought.

## MOTHER AND SON

At that moment, how we laughed,
each squeal infecting the other
as we struggled to recover.
Uncontrollably, ludicrously daft.

The ecstasy we wept, unrestrained.
Quivering chests heaving with glee.
The freeing laughter of juvenility.
Mine, then. Yours, now.
A portal in time
when our aspects aligned.
A beautiful feckless fools' domain.

My darling boy,
how I adored you.
A cascade of joy
lifting the heavy hue.
Happiness remembered.
Save, replay, enjoy.
So breezily unaware
of the ease that you bring.
A sorrow soothing hymn,
a saving answered prayer.

Aching bellies and bodies folded.
Gasping for air in between
choking chuckles,
our bliss beautifully moulded.
The air asinine
as our legs buckle.
A pocket of elation,
a keepsake of mine
where memories convene.

## THE IMPOSTOR

In the rooms that twinkle with crystal and opulence,
the women with Modigliani necks,
Bejewelled and bedecked
talking about young skin, exercise, and nutrition,
of flamboyant designers, fashionably Parisian.
Camouflaged, complacent corpulence.

Men in Armani suits and Swiss watches
consuming business with malt whisky.
Anecdotes of St Moritz and Apres-Ski.
An arcade of silver-spooned swatches.

A spectre occupying the void
in hand-me-downs and Primark shoes,
a day tripper just passing through,
the type you usually avoid.

Hair, brittle and untamed
Face conveying time's inflictions
No fillers or Botox injections
Expression caged and contained.

The Cheshire cats who smile sweetly
tiptoeing around class discreetly.
A barrage of plummeting playing cards
as the Queen haughtily stands guard.
I inhabit my place completely.

The advantaged advancing out of isolation.
The fortunes that swell with predation.
I am the stranger
in my lady's chamber.

## ODE TO A BICYCLE

I never learnt to ride a bike
but once, I longed to whizz through air.
Bell ringing, ribbons of windswept hair.
I think one day I might.

Mum said, "bikes are not for girls.
A good girl's legs politely furl."
Good girls aren't free.
Cultural captivity.

Then later I discovered
bikes are not for hymens
is what she really meant.
Even back then,
Silently dormant.
A commodity, undiscovered.

The jingle of Daisy Daisy
of a bike ride on a lazy,
vestal, Sunday afternoon.
When all the world is abloom.
I contemplate that maybe,
It is not the bike.

## BREASTS

Translucently delicate.
Finely sculptured orbs
Drooping
forbidden fruit.
Jiggling with each wiggle.
Cupping your fate.

Nuzzled
suckling cheeks,
enveloped in the fragrance
of talcum powdered womb.
Guzzled
liquid nurture,
binding.

Drawing glances
in a low-cut top.
A lover's face
buried
in their fleshy down.
Idolised,
objectified.
Gazing jouissance.

In public, feeding.
The eyes of scorn.
Touted
on the products
they adorn.
Their standards, grieving.

In the bathroom,
dreading
and hoping.

Frantically groping.
The life giver.
The lady killer
waiting
with impending doom.

You are blooming beauty.
You are the menacing beast.
Sagging, and
deflating with time
as the odds decline.
Athena's blooms
wilting fatally,
gasping for time
or cut with saving cruelty.

## LI'L BIG MAN

Injury during lockdown.
The son who looks like a man.
"Put your weight on me"
and how the tables turn.
That I should lean on you,
hobbling to A&E.
No money for taxis,
Saddled spectres in a ghost town.

Shouldering my weight without complaint
your words, a distraction from the pain.
I blessed you,
the child I grew,
my arm clenched around your frame.

In the waiting room, an age of arduous hours.
Squeaking nurse's shoes and eyes on devices.
Mingled with the masked buzz of voices.
Lockdown has no power over the injured
Pains that refuse to be hindered.
A vacuum where wounded gloom flowers.

A selfless gift of time.
Championed
by the child I championed.
An act of kindness.
To love and be loved.
The ties that bind.

## EQUILIBRIUM

Chasing the inner peace trail
Conflicting cranial critique
Deflation and defeats
Nebulous nirvana travails.

The chattering loggias of the maladied mind
The heckling harangue it savagely assigns
Flares of alarm like pulsating lesions
Clutching the last sun of the season.

The wheat from the chaff, sifted
Your weightless particles, lifted
Sanctuary under a Cypress tree
A released Atlas, light and free.

Silence the mind and meditate.
Loosen the reins and marinate.
Inhale the ascent you seek,
Exhale the descent of defeat.

A frantic fever of urgency
A chiding, mocking insurgency.
Double glaze and insulate
your mental well-being.

Life's noise infiltrates
spiritual seeking.
An elusive unobtainable strand
waving from "the sorrowless land"
at the cracked smile of uncertainty.

## GRAND UNION CANAL

Crisp sunshine in October.
The shadows maintain their cold
and the open expanse embraces the light,
bubbling flares of midsummer merriment.

The billowing canal surface
alive with musical grace.
Shimmying content
beneath bridges meant
for friendship and Poohsticks.
The lofty rumblings of M40 acoustics.
Afternoon shadows predict
long, dark winters in heated abodes.

A party of pallbearing clouds
furtively congregate overhead.
The council of conclusion.
Summer's sighing diffusion.
Brisk blustering gusts,
setting the table for the winter spread.

Islets of weeping willows
wheezily whipping in the breeze.
The snatched voices of autumn conversing on air.
Circus top barges that flow with the fun of the fair.
Al fresco dining, clinking.
Leafy lament beneath the marquees.

Feral foliage pushing back against the paved path.
A doily frill of malachite leaves that recalls
family mallow-picking's bountiful hauls.
Prepped and seasoned with North African craft.

The threat of winter, bluntly invasive.
Urban hibernation in the wings.
The forlorn farewell summer sings,
melodiously familiar and plaintive.


**THE UNMOORED MOOR**

In the scorched Arab peninsula
The brotherhood faces the kabla.
The oil field runneth over.
I am the poor relation.
Too African to qualify.

In Sub-Saharan Africa
where the forests are shrinking.
In the mines, buried twinkling.
Scrambled Africa on toast
for the First World we host.
Rejected by the flock,
too Arab for Africa.

In the place of my birth.
The glutinous annals of power,
exploited labour devoured
without recourse.
A Trojan horse
foraging in riches unearthed.
A geographical accident of birth.

A square peg in an ethnic box.
Identity in a tick.
Which self to tick?
A nulidad's paradox.

## TIRED

So tired of all the hullabaloo,
the postured extolling
the political patrolling.
Pointless, servile scrolling.
A time stealing, void filling milieu.

So dejected by the disclosures.
The grim severity of each bulletin.
A bullet in. Broadcasting barbarity.
Endemic exposures
without closure.

So drained by demands,
the cumbersome obligations,
the guilt of expectations
of frail isolated relations'
clinging liver spotted hands.

A bitter admonition
of my own fraying mortality.
Life's breaking banality.
The inescapable finality.
Crumbling cognition.

So fatigued by the sleep
that refuses to come
as the hours clang on.
The respite my thoughts shun
until dawn's first cheep.

Vanishing into the beam
of golden shards of dreams
to awaken all alone.
Death, only ever our own.

## MELANCHOLY

Socialised browsing.
Scrolling past penury.
Neurosis with bogus sunshine.
Brought to you by Paroxetine.

Overwhelmingly weighed down.
The crippling sadness.
The unbearable consultations
of a mind, less.

Encouraged to share and talk.
I cannot bear my own darkness.
Why then, should another?
Barbed thoughts with gouging sharpness.
A minacious murder of crows
driving dreams back with a squawk.

A platter showcasing only the tastiest morsels.
Concealed calamities behind kitchen doors.
The critic's napkin tucked under his chins.
Crushed crumbs tumbling as he begins.
Choice cuts of the mental carousels.

Faraway faces asking, "How ARE you?"
Conflicted with your own tribulations.
Never wanting more than "fine."
Insulating your isolation.
The pleasantries we silently co-sign.

## I HAVE LOVED

I have loved this house
in its ordered disorder,
each room recalling an event.
The stories the walls espouse.

I have loved this street
when flames of Carnival livery
warmed like a steel-pan August sun
pulsing with island beats.

I have loved this Earth.
Her breathtaking brush strokes,
A rainbow cornucopia of life
beyond the numbing dearth.

I have loved its people.
The ones who made it good.
Those who inspired and lifted,
who restored faith in people.

I have loved.
Not like fairy tales or films.
Not a soulmate or the one.
But enough
to ease the trudge.

## FATHER

The laugh that was a boom,
reverberating along the room.
An infectious timbre,
inviting in its limber.

The tiny legs that race
to keep up with your pace.
Long determined strides.
Toddlers chasing the tides.

A rogue glint in your eye.
A winking star
 in a still sky.
Incorrigible. Unforgettable.

Treasured recollections,
misplaced or lost, in the deserted hallways
of your mind, resurfacing infrequently,
random sips of reunion.

Sliding on your shoes
as you once did for me.
Reminders of the day's events
when the mind fog disorients.

Beneath the shadow of disorder,
your flaws magnified.
And still, I mourn the man
innocence made warmer.

The man I believed you to be.
Your spiked edges blurred.
Maybe somewhere, you still exist.

## SICK CITY

A city sterilised
against humans.
Behind the glass.
Millions of eyes,
inside, looking out.
Witnessing
their constructs
continue without them.
Each in their bubble.
As the experts advised.

The vacant streets.
A whoosh from a solitary car.
The isolated patter of feet
shepherded by a golden
colonnade of streetlamps.
Dominating the landscape.

Human conceits.
The breath thief
from the Far East.
Robed in chaotic crisis.
Nature's parting kiss.

## MAPPING THE VOID

It is strange that one
should feel so empty
When the anatomy
 is stacked with life enabling components.
Where does one find the emptiness?

Does it reside in
The chambers of the heart?
Expanding with every slight
Until the seams tear apart.

Maybe in the lungs.
Asphyxiating the bronchioles.
Squeezing out breaths
As you gasp and wheeze.

Perhaps in the mind,
Laying waste to the limbic nodes.
Extinguishing sparks of hope
As you wade through the dark.

Where emptiness finds a home.
A thirsty drop trickling into the briny
Deep, swaying the tide of the sea.
Quenched by our humanity.

The shadows sustained by the light.
Sometimes crashing against shores.
Others, cooling our toes.
Occasionally rising like seafoam.

# THE BAT AND THE BALL

Waiting to be picked.
The popularity prefects
bringing relief or dread.
If you're from somewhere else
you won't be chosen unless
you can help them win.
My chances are slim.
I am nobody's first pick.

The eyes that replay
the intolerance served at home.
Hattie will choose me, she's a shoo-in
putting all her power behind the bat.
The ball's breaking impact as it soars
above their heads as light as air.

Hattie says "we gotta have each other's back.
We're all foreigners here."
Occasionally accepted as friends
until anger brings the bad words
reserved for the brown hordes
inspired by the angry man on TV. Canned laughter.
She says "Bun dat, take no crap! We are people too."

Dangling acceptance.
Playground power-plays that stalked the days.
The face of imperialism
mirrored in the shallow pool
of childhood schisms.
Hattie, a rapid dark streak.
bolting towards fourth base.
The bats from strong trunks
winning for endurance.

## LIMBO

Africa calling.
A convoy in the shadows.
Constant and ever-present.
A home but not a home.

Anointing my edges.
Still, I fit nowhere.

Here, my name is foreign
my appearance questioned –
"But where are you from,
originally?"
probes Goldilocks,
cornfields in her hair.

I have reconciled
with the damp, dark streets.
Pierced by dimples
of obtrusive,
artificial light
illuminating
an artificial pond.

The dry wit
and caustic humour.
The sarcasm.
The armour we wear.

The sleazy, sullied snickers
of bawdry backstreet jokes.
The women who reject
gazing at the floor.
Audaciously holding his stare.

The jangle of frenetic city life.
The busy lives of others
filtering into our busy breaths.
In the darkened alcoves
and desolate cubicles
of existence,
Sartre echoed
"You're in bad company."

The clattering coffee shops.
Amid sips of acrid Arabica.
The inane monologues
on current affairs.
Clandestine consultations,
a temporary respite,
Soaked in caffeine and butter pastries.

London calling.
Cosmopolitan and enthralling.

It is the home
of a lodger.
The key to the Kingdom
presenting the illusion
of belonging
without belonging.
The solitude as natural
as blinking.

There, my name is familiar.
My appearance
fusing with the dry alleyways
and whitewashed facades,
facing off a fierce sun.

In the hotchpotch pavement cafes

where, once, Ginsberg
and Jean Genet supped
on mint tea
where tolerance
is privately practised
but never publicly preached.

The lamb and cumin infused air
that coils and slithers
before reclining across your skin
like an impermeable veil.

The language of my ancestors
tinged with my Britishness.
My speech fluent yet betraying
as wide-eyed locals
chuckle, like a pacifying parent.
"You're not from here, are you?"

In the Medinas,
The night sky turns down the heat,
as families parade in their best attire.
Sunflower seeds whose saltiness fizzes
on the tongue.
Sugar roasted peanuts
washed down with canary iced lemonade.

The men who gawk belligerently.
Their eyes betraying
the indignity of
a shameless woman
who refuses to look away.

The crested clay tagines
joyously bubbling away.
Terracotta, fat, jolly uncles.

The enticing wisps of flavour,
the fragrance of l'enfance.
The Ganawa drum beats.
A throbbing pulse.
Dancing. Chanting. Healing.
A portal to the beloved,
On the wings of a trance.

A cultural hub
that captivates and offends.

A shared identity.
An organic pond, rich with community.
Kindness. Support. Love.
"To serve is to be with Allah."

The allotted roles,
deeming marriage and its fruits,
the paragon of ambition.
Gender hindered.
Scornful eyes from the arbiters
of decency as I light my cigarette.

I am without decency
and without God.
Casting off the shackles of both.
The dogma of belief or illusion.
In the clutches of tradition,
Bleeding bequeathed injury.
Spurred on by my scars.

"You're not from here, are you?"
The cross of the diaspora.
Life's longing for the other.
Each suit offering some comfort
but ill fitting, nonetheless.

## THE DAYS

Back in my day.
We didn't concern ourselves
with the day.

Back when music was good.
We didn't consider if it was good
it just felt good.

Back when people had values
we didn't see the value
of the undervalued.

Back when children were safe.
We didn't see the danger
as they silenced the unsafe.

Back in the good old days.
We were the good
witnessing racism cloud the days.

Back in the days of real women.
Never occurring they could be more.
His story, hindering the real women.

Back in the days of real men.
Commended for silent strength.
A brave face censoring the real man.

Back when we had traditions.
Keeping things in the closet
as we submitted to tradition.

Today, hurt by time's disarray.
Each, accusing the other of change.
Yesterday's colours running into today.

**CHRISTMAS PRESENT**

Each, creating a home of sorts,
their substance ingrained in its walls
where contented comfort resides
releasing the self who hides.

Homes celebrating Diwali,
their faces glazed with light.
Families gathering for Eid,
a joyous celebratory feed.

In one residence a cat observes
from under a Christmas tree
his eyes flickering merrily,
his companion supping on tea.

A place enamoured with Christmas.
A chance to catch a little Christmas.
A shimmering tree in a Muslim home.
Milk and cookies in a Jewish one.
A letter to the North Pole
from a home with no God.

The contrasting dinners,
each reflecting a culture.
A feast of Caribbean splendour
as Wray and Nephew come to call,
lubricating the laughter.

A traditional turkey dinner,
frayed paper frills on its shins.
The tart heart of cranberry
pulses in the air with a zing.
Crackers shimmer gold
on the praising faces who gather.

A silent night at home
where one eats alone.
Switching channels
when the merriment hurts.
He resentfully asserts
the season to be nothing less
than the wet dream of capitalists.

Millions of dwellings
sharing love and glad tidings.
The ones without a manger
look into the goldfish bowl.
Rubbing themselves to keep warm.

"So, this is Christmas
and what have you done?"

Happy Christmas, war rages on.

# THE TATE

In The Tate on my tod.
A collage of observers lazily oozes
through the masters and their muses.
A spill of nodding dogs.

Curbed conversations
knell hollowly.
Une cage de la folie.
Captured culture
in gold Baroque frames.

Suckling on past glories,
inspired by their beauty,
Civilised groupies -
the modern-day bourgeoisie.

A painted gaze,
Escorting you around the room.
Gushing expression.
Lingering question.
Time, in her elected costumes.

A reassuring testimony
of the grace in us all.
Suffocated and stalled
in a consumer's ceremony.

A place of restful rumination.
Where still lifes still discontent
and the rich colours warm,
where dissociation
finds the art of quelling separation.

## DILUTED

I do not believe
as my grandparents did.
Like my parents believe.
But as my children don't.
Though one believes.

Losing my Moroccan.
Defeatedly dwindling.
Gradually ebbing away
until one day
no one will remember
Moroccan in the family.

My name is of the motherland
like my children's.
Their children's, maybe not.
The children's children
will have names that
nobody asks about.

My children do not speak
my grandparent's tongue.
Will my own Darija
flee from recall
overpowered by English
or will it linger
like Qandisha's kiss
signalling the end?

The presence of Morocco filtered out.
The future, unaware.
The North African sun
that smiles on them.
Occasionally, a throwback appearance.

The girl with Morocco in her eyes.
The boy with Picholine olive skin.

I hold my teapot high.
The mint tea dribbles
and babbles as it hits
the gold rimmed teacups.
Pan fried bread and trays of nuts,
sticky baklava soaking up
mint and orange blossom water.
Beautifying the warmth.

My descendants
will drink weak tea whilst dipping a Hobnob.
They will grimace at the mention
of parsley or coriander
and eat Moroccan in a restaurant.

In some respects, less than the women before,
in others, I am abundantly more.

But it is no great matter.
The little traditions and customs
we cling to, are nothing more
than taught belonging.
Ancestral peer pressure
For my identity to be yours
when all the things that make us
are as fleeting as we.

## WHEN THEY WERE YOUNG

Rucksacks tossed on the floor
Shoes obstructing the hallway.
Impatient hands make a grab
for the snack cupboard.
"Uniforms off first!"

Pint-sized limbs thunder down the stairs,
Full of chatter and mirth.
I longed for time.
Time to be the other me.

A time to mingle and socialise,
to fiercely protest and vocalise,
to dance the night away
come home at the break of day.

A nod to the irresponsible me.
No school runs to run your day.
In the driving seat instead.
A road trip to self discovery.

All the energy and none of the time.
Grasping sand to be left with the grains.
Plan for a day when time's demand wanes.
A time when time is on your hands.

All the time and none of the energy.
Shoes neatly stored in the shoe rack.
School's out so the teachers kick back.
Infecund classrooms and lethargy.

The reserve is sluggish and spent.
No will for idle chat or the idiocy it exposes.
The mind willing to dance, the body opposes.

To protest now, inefficient.
No toy hands diving into the fruit bowl.
The waxy oranges, undisturbed.
The longed-for order, unperturbed.
Order to make order of losing control.

## RECONCILIATION

The brother,
not a word spoken in years.
The weight of a matured grudge
finally laid down.
In the face of frailty,
she cannot cling to her injury.

Eyes flicker recognition
though neither is the same.
They have been estranged,
their presence unchanged.
Brother and sister
meeting in the winter.
He pulls her into his embrace.
The pain of years of animosity
Clouding his eyes.

An entreating gape bulging
out of a skeletal frame.
A disinfectant tinge hovers
intermingling
with lingering surrender.
Struck down in a stroke.

His speech, laboured.
His tongue weighed down.
She understands.
Pleas for home.
The food mirroring
the sterile emptiness.
The lifeless limbs
imprisoning him
from ability and home.

Indignant that her brother is abandoned
in death's waiting room. Gather
the children. Transform
"An impractical living space"
into the only practical place.

The affection locked off,
flooding back in seismic waves.
Grievances swept away.
The tragedy, only calamity
could prompt clemency.

## I AM NOT BERBER

I am not a Berber, the barbarian
of Greek Generals or the Roman raiders,
cowering in dust, conquered and crushed
by the illegitimate invaders
marauding coveted minerals
advancing your empires further.

The enemies at the gate.
The carpeted caliphates.
A pie divided in two.
"Half for me and half for you."
"Gracias, Merci, Adieu!"

I am a powerful Amazigh
who has smirked at adversity
for thousands of years,
flicking dusty tears.
Sipping warm mint tea
as Syrah dripped from the wounds
of the nomad fraternity.
Rising stronger from the debris.

My tongue peppered with Arabic,
French and Spanish.
Souvenirs I cannot vanquish.
My words an oral history
of defeat and victory,
immersed in rhythmic Maghreb music.

I cannot be erased or silenced
by the creed of the conquerors
with their patriarchal parlance.
I am of Al Kahina and conjurors.
A matriarchal Warrior Queen.

Neither faith nor power can defeat
a heart forged in desert heat.
Beware my spectacular spleen.

Sands scattered by the winds.
I travel across the globe
in Al-Maghreb woven robes
and olive grove skin.

One day you will say Berber
and I will see our ancestors,
the civilised and the barbarian.
The Amazigh and the Invader.
The jailer and liberty's Dame.
I will face you with fervour
as I assume my majestic role.

Hear my ululations
rising above tribulation
throughout history.
I am Amazigh.

## WHERE THE BIRDS DON'T FLY

The places where buildings crumble like sandcastles.
The sky coloured ashen
with explosive residue.
Where the sacrificial lambs wage power's battles.

The borders flooded by the advancing tides,
rushing towards safer sands,
propelled by a hostile surge.
Taking only their frantically bagged lives.

The homes where sirens turn the blood cold.
The blasts, increasingly louder.
Young fearfully, questioning eyes
find no answers. Strategic chaos takes hold.

In the ruins where the tears run dry.
Reclaim the dead from the debris.
Only the dead are free.
Without a song where the birds don't fly.

# ROUND TRIP

Bowie on the radio with the Young Americans.
The children of Woodstock
dancing to Glam Rock.
The new kids on the block,
here to hamper the old guard's plans.

The children of the revolution
flipping over tables.
Emerging out of the sable
of the shadow of war
and the values of yore
with tie-dyed solutions.

A jubilant generation X.
Born into free love and contraception.
Consciously tripping on introspection.
Parading placards to the apex.

Now the cat with the cream, tabling corporations.
Completely immersed.
Putting America First.
Free love, grubbily immoral.
Drugs, the sin of the amoral.
Begrudging in Maga hats.
Rejecting the "fake" facts.
The tangerine "new" old guard of the grump generation.

Angry anarchist to judge.
Once believing and idealistic.
Now disbelieving and "realistic".
Their boozed noses purple
as they come full circle.
Disillusioned and resentful.
Conservative and fundamental.

Spewing sanctimonious scorn.
"Where have all our heroes gone?"
Nursing a grey diseased grudge.

An ill wind of blustery blather
rolls over the matters that matter.
Obedient old Americans
silencing young Americans.

## BREWING OVER A BREW

In my worn robe, gazing into the cold tea dregs
fermenting in the bottom of a chipped mug,
feeling like somebody pulled the rug.
Silencing thought and the questions it begs.

If I was not here.
If I was nowhere, non-existent.
The question persistent.

An element in mist.
Would I miss it?
The children who anchor me,
baby fingers holding on tightly.
Would they hate and berate me?
Would they say I was selfish?
The spoon ran away from the dish.
Each memory sullied with tragedy.
An existence turned to shit.

The parents who outlived their child.
Could they forgive the ultimate sin?
Masking grief as they push out their chin.
Stumbling on without a crutch.
The hurt, their shame, corrupts.
My name loved and reviled.

Absently gulping cold dishwater sips.
Comforted by the TV's lulling noise.
The chicanery solitude employs,
suckling threadbare hope in drabs and drips!

I am not here or anywhere.
But I exist and life persists
seasoned with all I hold dear.

## RESURFACING

The crowds lined up, one after the other.
Hand sanitizer, squirt and smother.
Each hand furiously cleaning the other.

Each face, masked in defence.
Their eyes, cautiously intense.
Social distancing fully applied.
Braving the Covid tide.

Hand sanitizer stands, abandoned.
People stream past in a hurry.
Unburdened of previous worry.
A jab with the magic wand.
Social distance, casually shunned.

Face masks tucked into pockets.
To reach for if need be.
Their owners, breathing free.
A shabby Corona docket.

The sense of a frail security.
A patched-up boat
before the storm.
A mutated swarm.
A state of confused uncertainty.

# AUNTY

That chill, sprawling night in October, she passed.
Cradling the phone to my heart,
mourning a matriarch from my past,
the painful loss of an esteemed elder.

Beneath the shadow of Trellick Tower.
A quiet, close-knit street.
Faces of the community stop and greet
warmly embracing, kissing cheek to cheek.
Hijabed clusters, solemn and dour.

A bloom's lost recall of the fingers
whose determined toil
doggedly nurtured the soil
for future crops. A bustling copse
exploding with fruit from the briar.
Caged efflorescence, reaching higher.
Trailblazing a trail that still lingers.

A bronze hourglass figure
who always made time,
kindling the space with her shine.
Old school but modern of mind.
A spirit that none could shackle.
Head thrown back in joyous cackle.
Each elation filled with vigour.

The first generation planted in the cold.
Where the reception matched the freeze.
Enoch Powell and Doctor Martin disease.
"Bloody foreigners" hatefully spat.
They called their own expats.
Finding fellowship on Golborne Road.

The clapback of a whip,
Cracking quickfire quips.
The long working hours
and children she missed.
The better life she selflessly gifts
as her strength soundlessly slips.

The community she'd serve and assist.
Letters of the illiterate translated.
Rights and laws related
to the newly arrived uninitiated.
Her kind support, clearing the mist.

A generation who will never know
the stalwart who came before,
the courage she fought to bestow.

Then came the fatigue of long Covid.
Begrudgingly bound to her bed.
A Moroccan mosaic in her head.
Drained of the life force she embodied
as the carers questioned and prodded.
The fractured community that no longer calls.
The devoted daughter and granddaughters
warming the bleak four walls.
A testament of the good that she did.

Heartbroken by the cost.
The death of a familiar era.
In sepia memories, I free her.

## GARDEN VIEW

The quiet calm out here
when the world is shut down
and the breaths of sound
frost in the cold silent air.

Amber top windows in a silhouetted house
warm the dark. A plume of gold sparks
slips into the night like an amorous spouse.

Both windows lit by Chinese lanterns.
A vigil of luminous stares
gazing fondly at human tears
knowing at any time fortunes could turn.

Twitching curtains coyly wink.
Outstretched twiggy arms, reaching.
Their longing for light beseeches.
Crisp fingers clutching at life's twinkling.

The darkened windows below.
Cloaked in feral bushes.
A black, veined mesh pushes
against the light's intrusive glow.

Inky foliage figures stencilled on black.
Rough winds crackle and stir.
Open-palmed leaves audibly cheer.
Midnight's sentry is braced for attack.

The agile relevé of feline shadows
skip on moss-peaked garden sheds.
Gaunt branches curl round them in threads.
Civet tiptoes along the hedge.

A roof in assorted chimney top hats
each with spindly aerial arms.
looming over the eerie calm.
Matchstick soldiers in ghostly combat.

In the black
the mind pollutes the track
concealing the way back.
Bending, as a relenting resolve cracks.

Shadows and their masters join forces
covertly colluding with the night,
dominating, dismantling the light.
An onyx temporary respite
putting to bed human life, and its discourses.

## VENUS DE LA MENOPAUSIA

She sits.
The coal, shrinking from the flame.
Watercolours of radiance,
Spilling down her cheeks.
She wilts.

Camouflaging the roots,
exposed by the tides of time.
Colouring outside the lines.
The Emperor's new suit.

Her brush strokes paling.
Flight from the barren land.
Opaque blooms of nothingness.
The final unveiling.

Twisting the garments
until their dyes run out.
The fabric worn,
washed up and washed out.
Hung out to dry.

Battered by the wind.
Still, clinging to the line.
To let go is
to drop the kite's string.

Life chiselled into sculpture.
Each fleshy flaw, amplified.
The spotlight abaft.
A woman unmasked.
Venus, put out to pasture.

**SISTER**

A happy place between cultures
Far from fear and expectation.
Hushed tones under the bed covers,
Dreams told with minstrel oration.

Each high and low perfumed
With your essence.
Triumph and failure, fine tuned.
The delicate touch of a pianist.

Lost in the pages of Narnia tales.
Heartily roused and regaled.
Drip-fed your steady voice,
Devouring every word.
Taking our thrones at Cair Paravel,
Breaking the White Witch's spell.
The resplendent dreams fantasy hails.

A lifeline
Through the trials of adolescence.
Honey and lemon pancakes,
Their spice, disarming the darkness.
Home.

## WRITING ON REEFER

The tap-tap of keyboards.
Trails spill from the mind.
Imagination ablaze.
A brainstorming haze.
Ideas plucked and refined.

Thoughts and words interweave.
The block, dissolving.
Expression, evolving.
Kerouac emerging from the weeds.

Infrequent gulps of dark, sharp sourness.
Sickly sweet with a dash of cream.
A tug at the conscious stream.
Snowy ribbons drift up to the cornice.

A searing marigold flare.
The subconscious seeping out of confinement,
To chart and captain the assignment,
Drifting with the flow of the flair.

Singing "Life is but a dream."
Syphoning the heart of emotion.
Bleeding in eloquent motion.
Born of flight of fancy's gleam.

Times New Roman, castigating on white.
Je t'accuse. I muse,
Plucking strands of psyche for my playful delight.

"The moving finger writes, and having writ"
Lands the plane on the strip.
Doused in earthy Colombian sips.
Mulling over the letters the mind submits.

**FOODBANK**

In the rooms where we make parcels.
Stacked up tins and non-perishables.
When the virus has hit hard and morale is scarred
We struggle to hold all our marbles.

Tailored bags, veggie or meat eater.
Selecting each item with loving care.
Feeding the families without a prayer
in the house of the stained-glass-eyed preacher.

My ties with Islamic culture,
Cater to the tastes of the ummah
in accordance with their sunnah.
Dignity beneath the vultures.

Gluten free treats for the children.
A chocolate for mum
to sweeten the glum.
Community alms in the temple den.

Plant based milk for the vegans.
Generous with pulses and pasta.
Queues at the door as we pack faster.
The dejected flocking to the subsistence haven.

The excitement of something nice.
M & S biscuits or a Waitrose dessert.
The priceless small pick me ups we insert.
A leg up for basic human rights.

Outside the lofty rose window
a clattering of jackdaws noisily caw.
Premade bundles conceal the storeroom floor.
Misfortune offers no furlough.

Protein for the meat eaters,
Beef curry or steak and kidney pie.
Taste the orient, a chicken Pad Thai.
Ignored by carnivorous leaders.

A fairy cake, home baking kit
for quality time with the family.
Amid poverty, making memories.
The smell of baking comforting the kids.

Those already acquainted with nothing
and those who have lost it all
filing into the hallowed hall.
The hurt of the broken calls,
sometimes, thankful and others, biting.

Each of us, one pay cheque away from destitution.
There but for the grace of God...
The God with a punishing rod.
Party politics offers no divine restitution.

## CLOCKING OUT MUM

Shared parting words at the door
choked by the breach of my heart.
The son, about to depart.
Life, in a case on the floor.

A fresh start in the Far East, away
from acquaintance with the clandestine
paths where the soul deviates, chances decline.
No more stop and search on the street.

A blank canvas to sagely brocade.
A leap I never could take.
The familiar, too high a stake.
Where nobody knows your name.
No record to reject or shame.
Into the sun and out of the shade.

"I love you mum."
Smiling as you waved.
You made the choice that saved
from incarceration or the grave.
The hurt I tenderly forgave.
Muted loss, etched on my face.
My shift, done.

The world's heavens are closed.
Stored love has no place to go.
A mother reminisces
on the child she misses.
A thought in the absence imposed.

www.ingramcontent.com/pod-product-compliance
Lightning Source LLC
Chambersburg PA
CBHW030311100526
44590CB00012B/598